CONSEQUENTIAL
DILEMMAS

KNOCK
KNOCK®
VENICE, CALIFORNIA

Created, published, and distributed by Knock Knock
1635-B Electric Ave.
Venice, CA 90291
knockknockstuff.com
Knock Knock is a registered trademark of Knock Knock LLC

This book is a work of editorial nonfiction meant solely for entertainment purposes.
It is not intended to advocate any particular course of action in any situation. It is also
not intended to diagnose or treat any psychiatric, psychological, emotional, or physical
problem. Following the directives indicated in this book would not only be tragically
literal, it could also be illegal, immoral, or downright dangerous. In no event will
Knock Knock be liable to any reader for any damages, including direct, indirect,
incidental, special, consequential, or punitive damages, arising out of or in connection
with the use of the information contained in this book. So, you know, lighten up.

ISBN: 978-160106850-7
UPC: 825703-50226-8

10 9 8 7 6 5 4 3 2 1

TABLE OF CONTENTS

INTRODUCTION

Should you get married? Have a child? Drink at work? These are big questions no one else can answer for you.

But a flowchart can.

Sometimes you may want two different outcomes at the same time—*I'd like to drink at my job. I'd also like to keep my job.* Other times you may be unsure of a decision because its possible outcomes are unknowable—on the leap-of-faith scale, *Should I have a child?* is basically the same as *Should I join the first human mission to Mars?* Perhaps you're stuck because you're simply standing too close to a problem. In all these cases, flowcharts provide a visual version of echolocation, giving an outline of the shape and boundaries of a dilemma—and of your feelings about it. All around us is chaos, yet flowcharts provide a sense of structure. Really good ones can even provide answers.

Flowcharts have become a popular form of internet meme in recent times, but the form has remarkably old, nerdy roots. Closely related to mathematical algorithms, flowcharts were used by pioneering computer coders in the 1940s, and by early industrial-efficiency experts in the 1920s. Some historians date the first flowchart to 1843, when Ada Lovelace composed an algorithm that is now considered the world's first computer program.

Whether you're an egghead or airhead, you can enjoy these charts' capacity to illuminate major life questions in their entirety, both as linear processes and holistic systems. Like engineers of the early 20th century, we remain enchanted by the form's ability to help us visualize and deal with the unpredictability of existence.

And if you're facing one of life's smaller—but no less puzzling—issues, consult this book's companion, *Inconsequential Dilemmas*, which offers guidance on daily conundrums including Halloween costumes, karaoke selections, and whether you should do laundry.

_Do I_

HATE
MY JOB?

DO YOU FIND YOURSELF OFTEN MUTTERING "I **LOVE** MY JOB" OVER AND OVER?

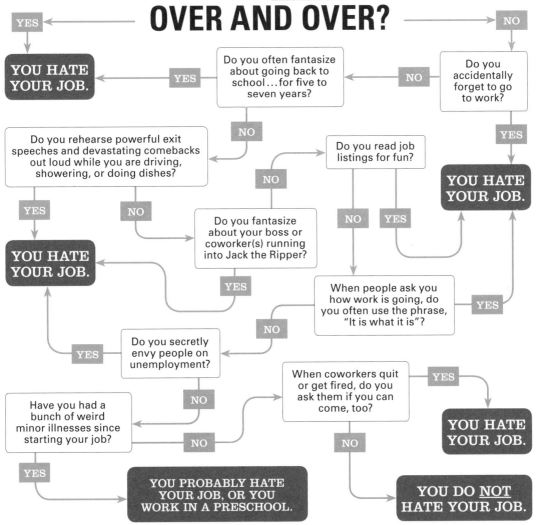

CAN I WEAR A CODPIECE?

ARE YOU IN A HEAVY METAL COMBO?

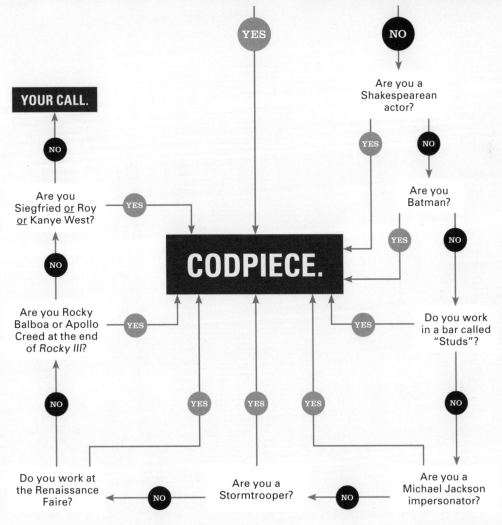

YES

NO

Are you a Shakespearean actor?

YES

NO

YOUR CALL.

NO

Are you Siegfried or Roy or Kanye West?

YES

Are you Batman?

YES

NO

NO

CODPIECE.

Are you Rocky Balboa or Apollo Creed at the end of *Rocky III*?

YES

YES

Do you work in a bar called "Studs"?

NO

NO

YES

YES

YES

YES

NO

Do you work at the Renaissance Faire?

NO

Are you a Stormtrooper?

NO

Are you a Michael Jackson impersonator?

SHOULD I BUY THIS HOUSE?

CAN YOU AFFORD IT?

11

SHOULD I USE THIS PORTA-POTTY?

WHAT IS THIS PORTA-POTTY'S MAJOR MALFUNCTION?

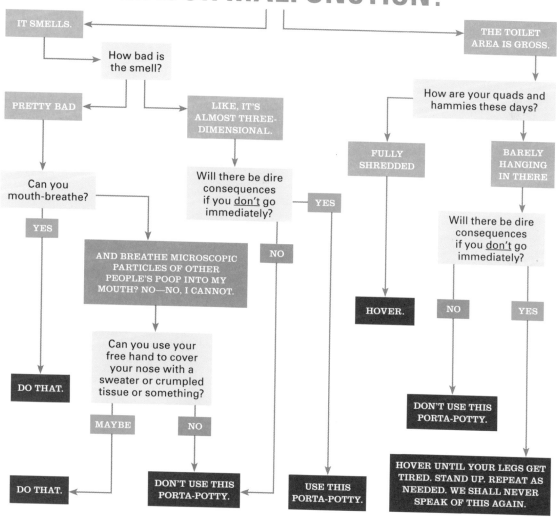

SHOULD I WRITE A MEMOIR?

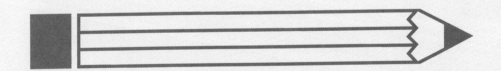

ARE YOU FAMOUS?

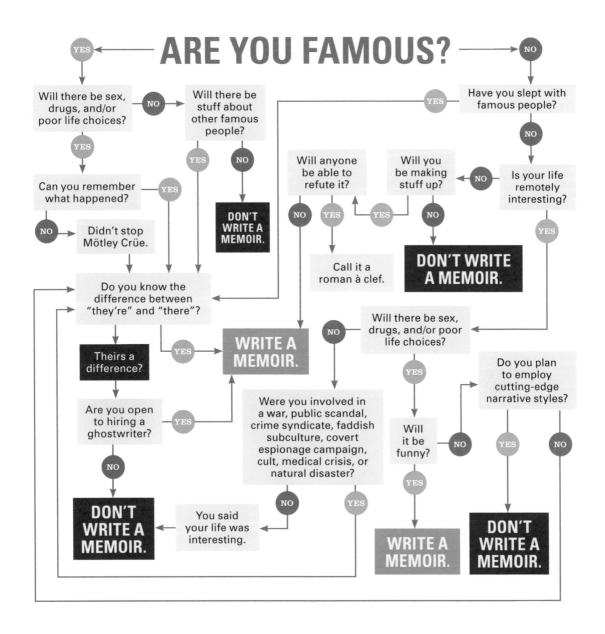

YES ← → NO

Will there be sex, drugs, and/or poor life choices?

NO → **Will there be stuff about other famous people?**

YES → **Have you slept with famous people?**

NO → **Is your life remotely interesting?**

YES ↓ Can you remember what happened?

YES → **Will anyone be able to refute it?**

Will you be making stuff up? ← NO

NO → Didn't stop Mötley Crüe.

YES → **Will there be stuff about other famous people?**

NO → **DON'T WRITE A MEMOIR.**

NO → **Do you know the difference between "they're" and "there"?**

NO → Call it a roman à clef. ← YES

NO → **DON'T WRITE A MEMOIR.**

YES → Theirs a difference?

YES → **WRITE A MEMOIR.**

NO → **Will there be sex, drugs, and/or poor life choices?**

YES → Do you plan to employ cutting-edge narrative styles?

Are you open to hiring a ghostwriter?

YES → Were you involved in a war, public scandal, crime syndicate, faddish subculture, covert espionage campaign, cult, medical crisis, or natural disaster?

YES → Will it be funny?

NO → **DON'T WRITE A MEMOIR.**

NO → You said your life was interesting. ← NO

YES → **WRITE A MEMOIR.**

YES → **WRITE A MEMOIR.**

NO → **DON'T WRITE A MEMOIR.**

—AM I A— HIPSTER?

17

SHOULD I

HAVE A KID?

CAN I DRINK AT WORK?

ARE YOU JAMES BOND?

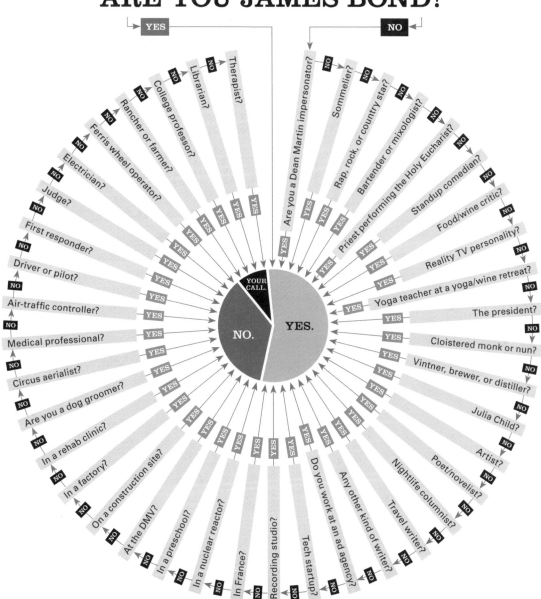

YES | **NO**

Therapist?
Librarian?
College professor?
Rancher or farmer?
Ferris wheel operator?
Electrician?
Judge?
First responder?
Driver or pilot?
Air-traffic controller?
Medical professional?
Circus aerialist?
Are you a dog groomer?
In a rehab clinic?
In a factory?
On a construction site?
At the DMV?
In a preschool?
In a nuclear reactor?
In France?
Recording studio?
Tech startup?
Do you work at an ad agency?
Any other kind of writer?
Travel writer?
Nightlife columnist?
Poet/novelist?
Artist?
Julia Child?
Vintner, brewer, or distiller?
Cloistered monk or nun?
The president?
Yoga teacher at a yoga/wine retreat?
Reality TV personality?
Food/wine critic?
Standup comedian?
Priest performing the Holy Eucharist?
Bartender or mixologist?
Rap, rock, or country star?
Sommelier?
Are you a Dean Martin impersonator?

YOUR CALL.
NO.
YES.

21

THERE'S A SEAT AVAILABLE IN THE EXIT ROW.
I REALLY WANT TO SIT IN THE EXIT ROW.

SHOULD I SIT IN THE EXIT ROW?

DO YOU MEET THE LIST OF REQUIREMENTS?

YES

NO

ALMOST

You should sit in the exit row.

SHOULD I MOVE IN WITH MY SIGNIFICANT OTHER?

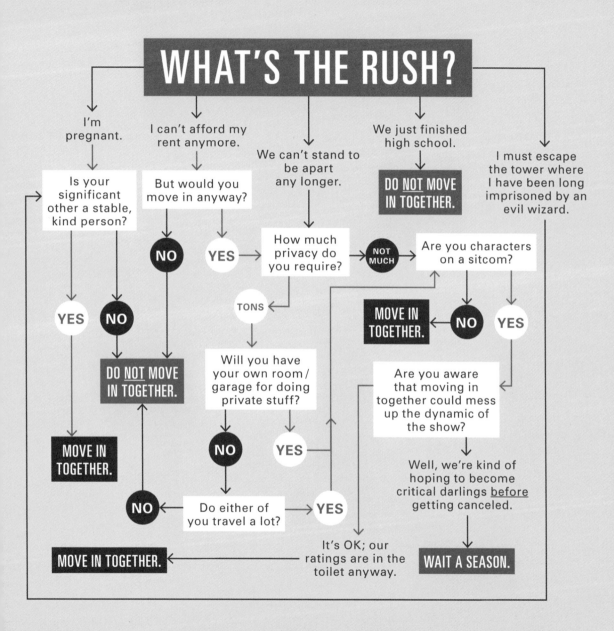

WHAT'S THE RUSH?

I'm pregnant.

I can't afford my rent anymore.

We can't stand to be apart any longer.

We just finished high school.

I must escape the tower where I have been long imprisoned by an evil wizard.

DO **NOT** MOVE IN TOGETHER.

Is your significant other a stable, kind person?

But would you move in anyway?

NO

YES

How much privacy do you require?

NOT MUCH

Are you characters on a sitcom?

YES

NO

TONS

MOVE IN TOGETHER.

NO

YES

Will you have your own room / garage for doing private stuff?

Are you aware that moving in together could mess up the dynamic of the show?

DO **NOT** MOVE IN TOGETHER.

NO

YES

Well, we're kind of hoping to become critical darlings before getting canceled.

MOVE IN TOGETHER.

NO

Do either of you travel a lot?

YES

It's OK; our ratings are in the toilet anyway.

WAIT A SEASON.

MOVE IN TOGETHER.

AM I A CAT LADY?

Do you do any kind of "crafting" with cat hair?

NO

YES—WHY? IS THAT WEIRD? → YOU ARE A CAT LADY.

Is your Facebook feed full of cats?

YES

NO

Do you live with a cat? ← NO ← Are they pictures of your cat? ← Check again. Everyone's Facebook feed is full of cats.

YES

NO YES → Do you have more than two cats? ← YES

Do you get excited when you see cats in movies?

YES NO

YES NO → Are you single?

Do you live on a farm? → YES

NO YES

Do you feed feral cats?

SORRY, YOU ARE NOT A CAT LADY.

SORRY, YOU ARE NOT A CAT LADY.

NO YES

Do people give you cat-themed mugs, magnets, or Christmas ornaments?

YOU ARE BECOMING A CAT LADY.

NO

YES NO

Wait, do you mean clothes with cats or for cats? → WITH

NO YES

FOR → YOU ARE A CAT LADY.

Do you have cat clothes?

SHOULD I STOP TRYING SO HARD?

ARE YOU AT WORK?

NO ← ARE YOU AT WORK? → **YES**

Are you on a date?

Couldn't someone else try so hard for you?

Can you stop trying so hard?

NO → Will you reveal how awesome you are? → **YES**

→ **MAYBE**

If you stop trying so hard, will you reveal how evil and/or boring you are? → **YES** → **DON'T STOP TRYING SO HARD.**

NO → **YES**

NO **YES** **YES** **NO**

START TRYING TO STOP TRYING SO HARD. → **BUT NOT TOO HARD.**

Are you watching children?

NO **YES** → Are these children family?

YES → **NO**

STOP TRYING SO HARD.

If you stop trying so hard, will anyone be permanently scarred? → **NO**

YES → Like, really really bad? → **NO**

DON'T STOP TRYING SO HARD.

YES → **YES**

Are you doing high-intensity interval training? → **NO** → Whatever you're doing, do you have a shot at fame and/or fortune? → **YES** → How much are we talking? A lot?

NO

NO

If you stop trying so hard will you lose your job?

NO → Do you care if you lose your job?

YES → **YES**

YES → **DON'T STOP TRYING SO HARD.**

YES

29

SHOULD WE GET THE BAND BACK TOGETHER?

DO YOU HAVE ANY FANS BESIDES YOUR FAMILIES?

NO

YES

Are you children?

NO

YES

GET THE BAND BACK TOGETHER.

DON'T GET THE BAND BACK TOGETHER.

NO

YES

Are you being offered tons of money to reunite at Coachella?

YES

NO

Do you hate each other?

YES

Are you embarrassed you were in the band?

NO

"HATE" IS A STRONG WORD.

YES

Are you guys fat and/or balding?

Was the band pretty bad, pretty good, or awesome?

PRETTY BAD

PRETTY GOOD

AWESOME

What percentage of the band is alive and not in treatment?

< 50%

> 50%

Are you prepared for the amount of drinking you'll have to do just to be in the same room with those jerks?

NOT REALLY

YES

GET THE BAND BACK TOGETHER.

GET THE BAND BACK TOGETHER.

Were you fat and/or balding when the band was together?

YES

NO

NO

Were you a 1960s/'70s family band?

NO

Can you get in shape/get hair?

YES

NO

YES

Were you guys awesome, pretty good, or pretty bad?

AWESOME

PRETTY GOOD

PRETTY BAD

DON'T GET THE BAND BACK TOGETHER.

Is the band's frontman/woman alive and not in treatment?

NO

YES

Will the band's reunion relieve the despair of a devastated mining town?

YES

NO

YOUR CALL.

GET THE BAND BACK TOGETHER.

31

ANNOYING?

DO YOU DO CROSSFIT?

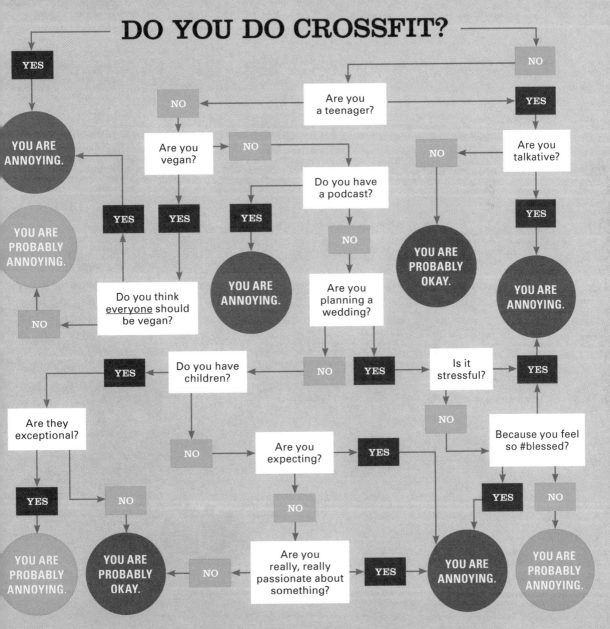

SHOULD I MARRY THIS PERSON?

Is this person boring?

YES

NO

Is this person honest?

NO

YES

Does this person "get" who you are and what you need to be happy—and manage to provide it much of the time?

NO

YES

So, they're loving and supportive and all that?

NO

YES

Can you imagine being super-happy without this person?

YES

NO

Does this person consider you the greatest, most precious, special person in the universe—and vice versa?

Does this person make your heart sing, and vice versa?

YES

NO

NO

YOU SHOULD NOT MARRY THIS PERSON.

YES

Do you want to have sex with this person for the rest of your life?

NO

YES

Does this person have a personality disorder or untreated addiction?

YES

NO

How long have you known each other?

2 weeks

< 2 years

> 2 years

YOU MAY GET ENGAGED.

Is one of you already married?

YES

NO

Do you guys have compatible views on money, religion, and Justin Bieber?

YES

YOU SHOULD MARRY THIS PERSON.

NO

DO COUPLES' COUNSELING FIRST.

SHOULD I GO OFF THE GRID?

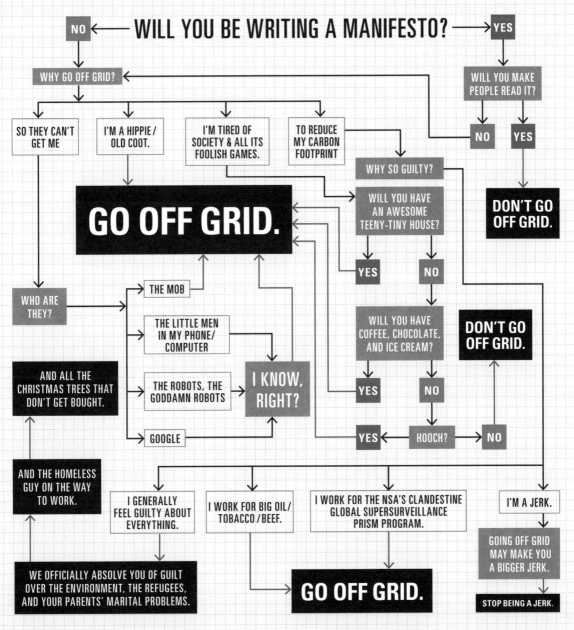

WILL YOU BE WRITING A MANIFESTO?

NO

YES

WHY GO OFF GRID?

WILL YOU MAKE PEOPLE READ IT?

NO

YES

SO THEY CAN'T GET ME

I'M A HIPPIE / OLD COOT.

I'M TIRED OF SOCIETY & ALL ITS FOOLISH GAMES.

TO REDUCE MY CARBON FOOTPRINT

WHY SO GUILTY?

DON'T GO OFF GRID.

GO OFF GRID.

WILL YOU HAVE AN AWESOME TEENY-TINY HOUSE?

YES

NO

WHO ARE THEY?

THE MOB

WILL YOU HAVE COFFEE, CHOCOLATE, AND ICE CREAM?

DON'T GO OFF GRID.

THE LITTLE MEN IN MY PHONE / COMPUTER

AND ALL THE CHRISTMAS TREES THAT DON'T GET BOUGHT.

THE ROBOTS, THE GODDAMN ROBOTS

I KNOW, RIGHT?

YES

NO

GOOGLE

YES

HOOCH?

NO

AND THE HOMELESS GUY ON THE WAY TO WORK.

I GENERALLY FEEL GUILTY ABOUT EVERYTHING.

I WORK FOR BIG OIL / TOBACCO / BEEF.

I WORK FOR THE NSA'S CLANDESTINE GLOBAL SUPERSURVEILLANCE PRISM PROGRAM.

I'M A JERK.

GOING OFF GRID MAY MAKE YOU A BIGGER JERK.

WE OFFICIALLY ABSOLVE YOU OF GUILT OVER THE ENVIRONMENT, THE REFUGEES, AND YOUR PARENTS' MARITAL PROBLEMS.

GO OFF GRID.

STOP BEING A JERK.

AM I WATCHING
GAME OF THRONES
OR
GILMORE GIRLS?

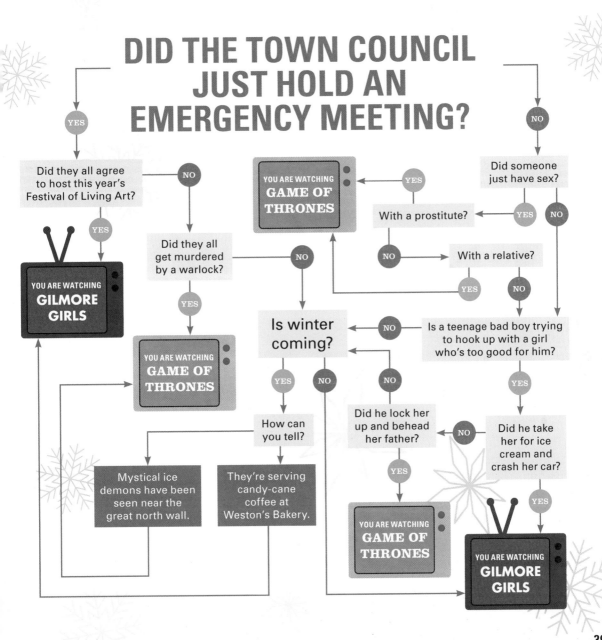

DID THE TOWN COUNCIL JUST HOLD AN EMERGENCY MEETING?

YES

Did they all agree to host this year's Festival of Living Art?

NO

YES

YOU ARE WATCHING GILMORE GIRLS

Did they all get murdered by a warlock?

YES

YOU ARE WATCHING GAME OF THRONES

NO

Is winter coming?

YES

How can you tell?

Mystical ice demons have been seen near the great north wall.

They're serving candy-cane coffee at Weston's Bakery.

NO

YOU ARE WATCHING GAME OF THRONES

YES

With a prostitute?

NO

With a relative?

YES

NO

Did someone just have sex?

YES

NO

Is a teenage bad boy trying to hook up with a girl who's too good for him?

NO

YES

Did he lock her up and behead her father?

NO

Did he take her for ice cream and crash her car?

YES

YOU ARE WATCHING GAME OF THRONES

YES

YOU ARE WATCHING GILMORE GIRLS

SHOULD I DO MY OWN ELECTRICAL REPAIRS?

ARE YOU AN ELECTRICIAN?

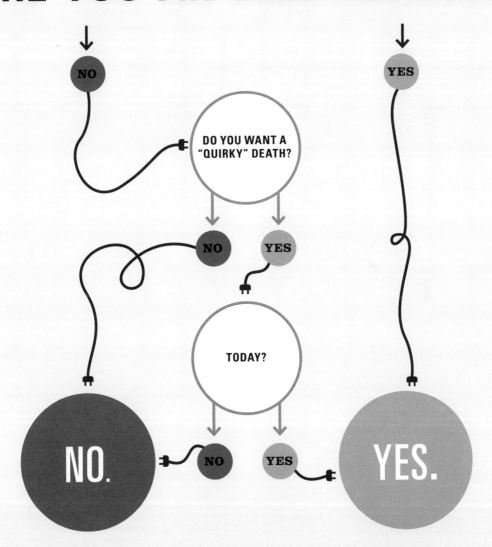

IS THIS PERSON TOXIC?

DOES THIS PERSON MAKE YOU FEEL LIKE EVERYTHING IS BAD, SAD, AND STUPID?

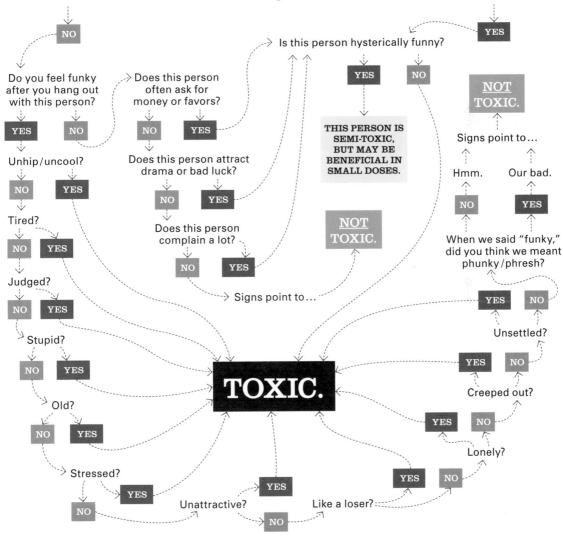

NO

Is this person hysterically funny?

YES

Do you feel funky after you hang out with this person?

Does this person often ask for money or favors?

YES

NO

NOT TOXIC.

YES   NO

THIS PERSON IS SEMI-TOXIC, BUT MAY BE BENEFICIAL IN SMALL DOSES.

Signs point to...

YES   NO

Unhip/uncool?

NO   YES

Does this person attract drama or bad luck?

Hmm.   Our bad.

NO   YES

NOT TOXIC.

Tired?

NO   YES

NO   YES

Does this person complain a lot?

When we said "funky," did you think we meant phunky/phresh?

Judged?

NO   YES

YES

NO   YES

YES   NO

Stupid?

Signs point to...

Unsettled?

NO   YES

YES   NO

Old?

TOXIC.

Creeped out?

NO   YES

YES   NO

Stressed?

Lonely?

YES

YES   NO

YES   NO

NO

Unattractive?

Like a loser?

NO

43

SHOULD I GO TO BURNING MAN?

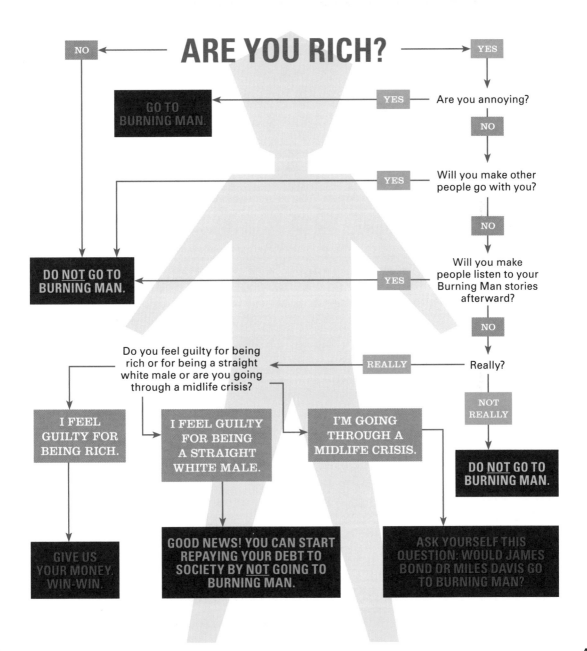

ARE YOU RICH?

NO ← → | → YES

Are you annoying? — YES → GO TO BURNING MAN.

NO ↓

Will you make other people go with you? — YES →

NO ↓

Will you make people listen to your Burning Man stories afterward? — YES → DO **NOT** GO TO BURNING MAN.

NO ↓

Really? — REALLY → Do you feel guilty for being rich or for being a straight white male or are you going through a midlife crisis?

NOT REALLY ↓

DO **NOT** GO TO BURNING MAN.

I FEEL GUILTY FOR BEING RICH. → GIVE US YOUR MONEY. WIN-WIN.

I FEEL GUILTY FOR BEING A STRAIGHT WHITE MALE. → GOOD NEWS! YOU CAN START REPAYING YOUR DEBT TO SOCIETY BY **NOT** GOING TO BURNING MAN.

I'M GOING THROUGH A MIDLIFE CRISIS. → ASK YOURSELF THIS QUESTION: WOULD JAMES BOND OR MILES DAVIS GO TO BURNING MAN?

SHOULD I READ THE COMMENTS AT THE END OF THIS ARTICLE?

Is the article about funny cats or no-sew reupholstery for ottomans?

YES

READ THE COMMENTS.

NO

Is the article about you?

YES

Is it about someone or something you have positive or negative feelings about?

NO

YES

DO NOT READ THE COMMENTS.

NO

Will you be tempted to respond to any of the comments?

YES

NO

REALLY

Really?

YES

Are you OK with misspellings, poor grammar, and Random capitalization?

NO

SERIOUSLY, REALLY. LIKE 99% REALLY.

DEFINATLY

Do you enjoy a basic faith in humanity?

NO

If you're so above it all, you really don't care what some loser commenters have to say, right?

Right?

HEY, WHERE'D YOU GO?

You're already reading them, aren't you.

Yeah, right. You are so totally going to respond.

SHOULD WE SPLIT UP TO COVER MORE GROUND?

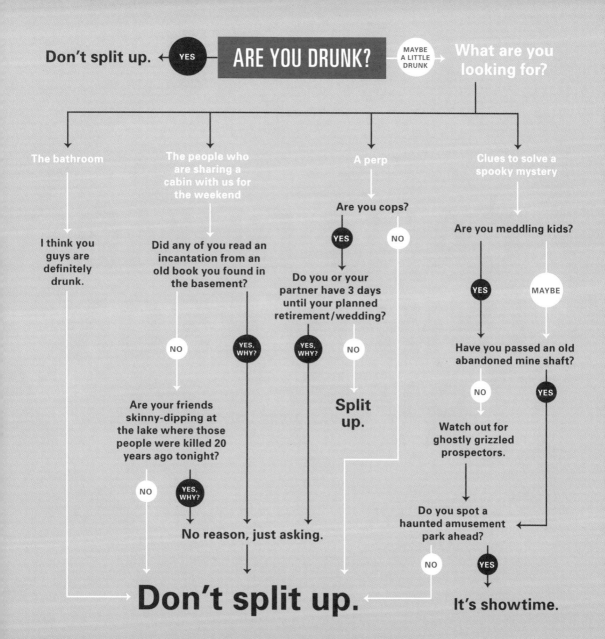

Don't split up. ← YES — **ARE YOU DRUNK?** — MAYBE A LITTLE DRUNK → What are you looking for?

The bathroom

I think you guys are definitely drunk.

The people who are sharing a cabin with us for the weekend

Did any of you read an incantation from an old book you found in the basement?

NO

Are your friends skinny-dipping at the lake where those people were killed 20 years ago tonight?

NO

YES, WHY?

YES, WHY?

No reason, just asking.

A perp

Are you cops?

YES

NO

Do you or your partner have 3 days until your planned retirement/wedding?

YES, WHY?

NO

Split up.

Clues to solve a spooky mystery

Are you meddling kids?

YES

MAYBE

Have you passed an old abandoned mine shaft?

NO

YES

Watch out for ghostly grizzled prospectors.

Do you spot a haunted amusement park ahead?

NO

YES

Don't split up. ←

It's showtime.

CAN I DUMP THIS PERSON BY TEXT?

Did you hang out more than three times?

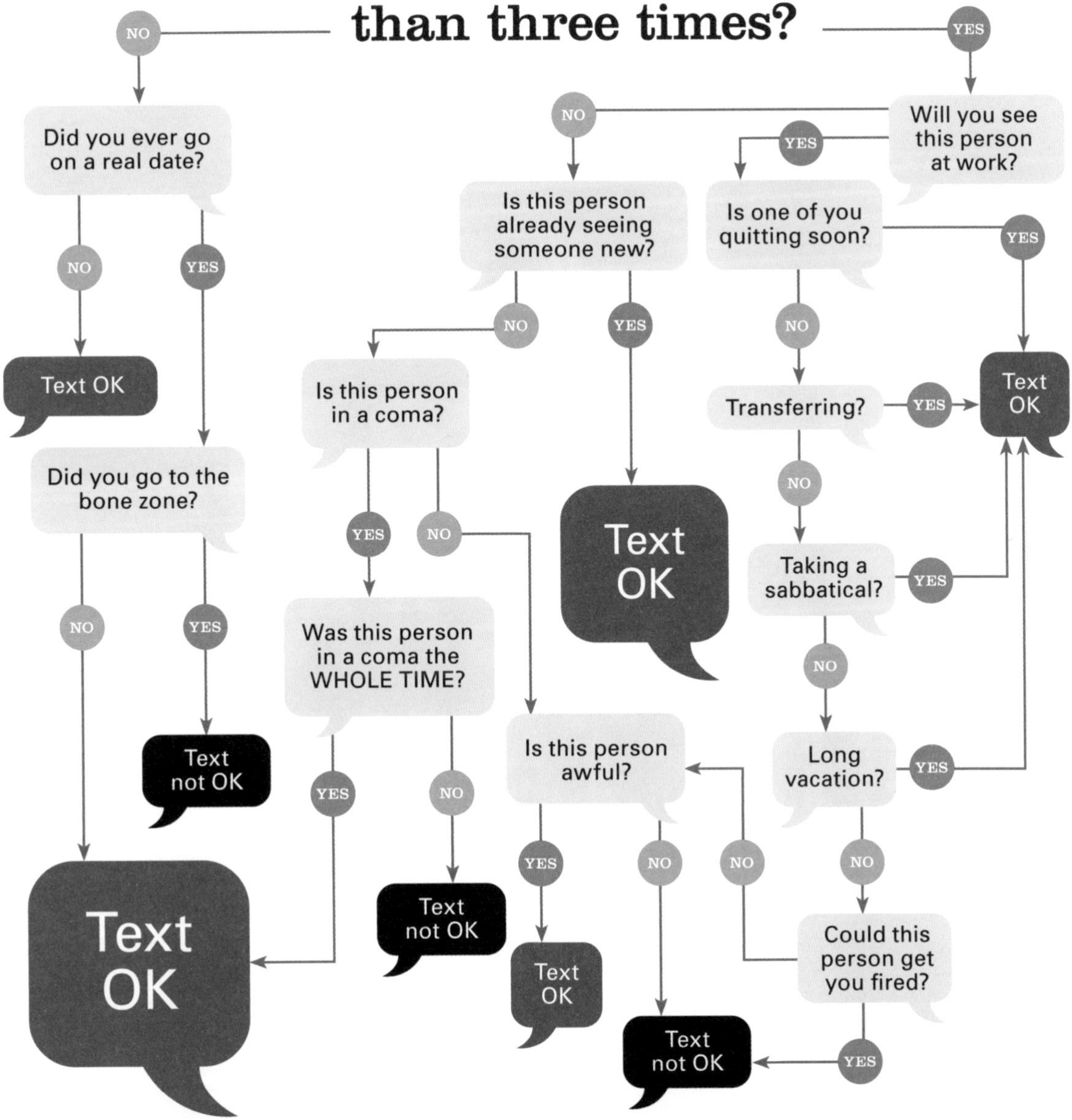

AM I A DEMOCRAT, REPUBLICAN, OR LIBERTARIAN?

JOHNNY CASH OR ELVIS PRESLEY?

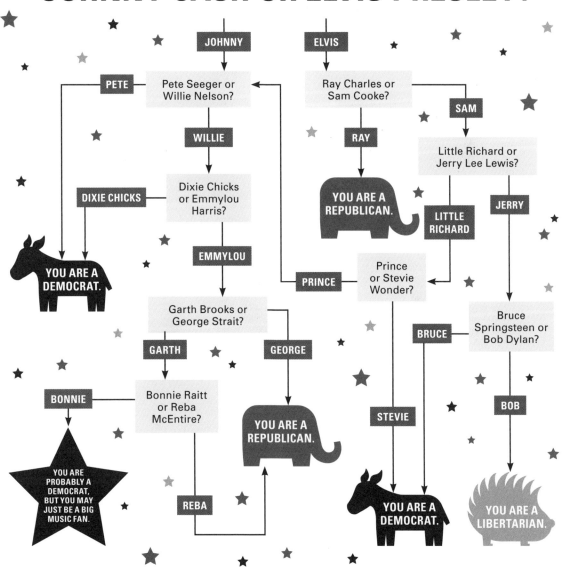

AM I A
SOCIOPATH?

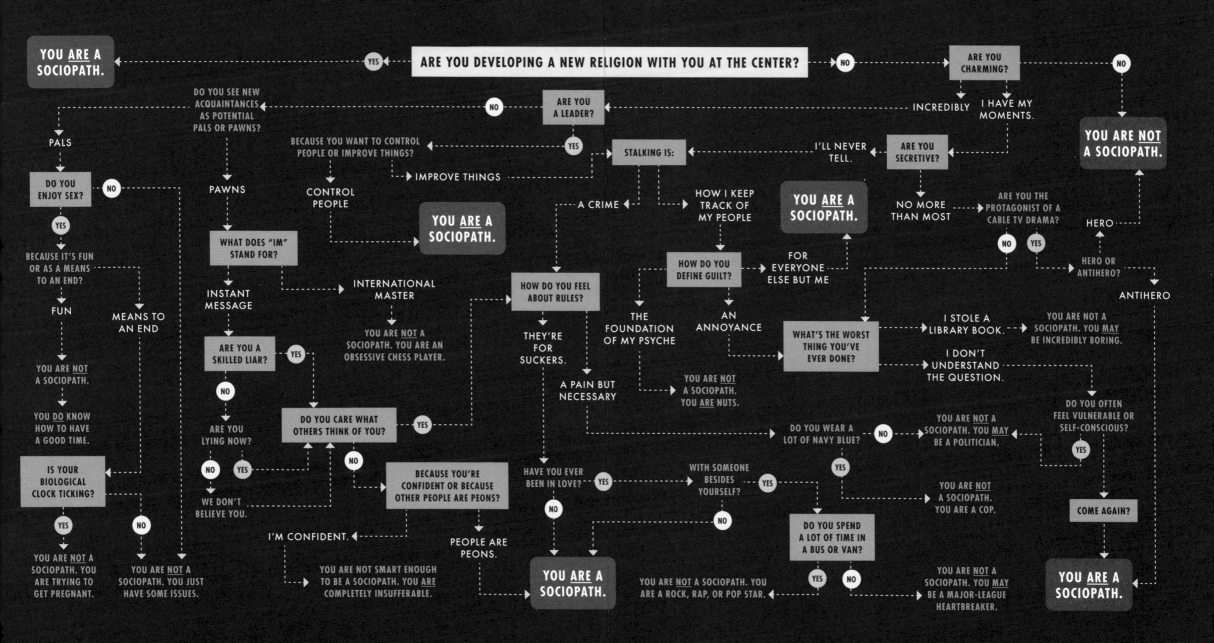

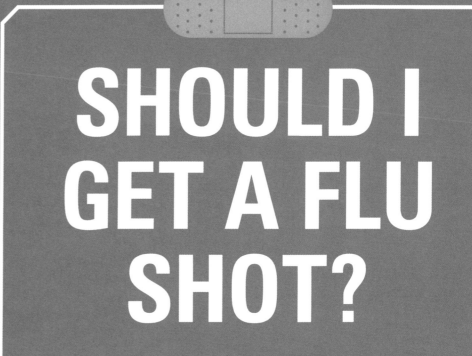

SHOULD I GET A FLU SHOT?

DO YOU KNOW ANYTHING ABOUT THE 1918 FLU PANDEMIC?

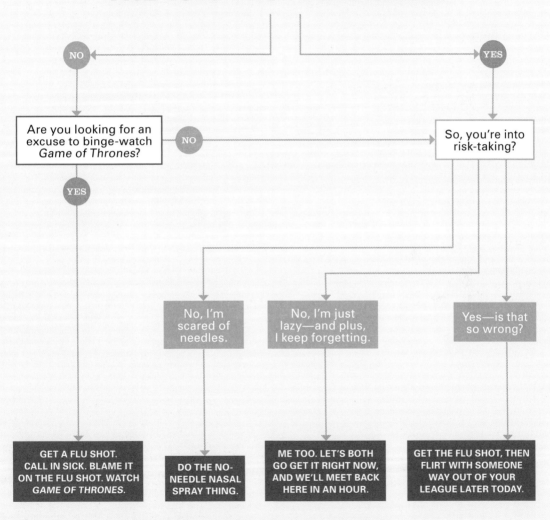

NO

YES

Are you looking for an excuse to binge-watch *Game of Thrones*?

NO

So, you're into risk-taking?

YES

No, I'm scared of needles.

No, I'm just lazy—and plus, I keep forgetting.

Yes—is that so wrong?

GET A FLU SHOT. CALL IN SICK. BLAME IT ON THE FLU SHOT. WATCH *GAME OF THRONES*.

DO THE NO-NEEDLE NASAL SPRAY THING.

ME TOO. LET'S BOTH GO GET IT RIGHT NOW, AND WE'LL MEET BACK HERE IN AN HOUR.

GET THE FLU SHOT, THEN FLIRT WITH SOMEONE WAY OUT OF YOUR LEAGUE LATER TODAY.

SHOULD I GET A DIVORCE?

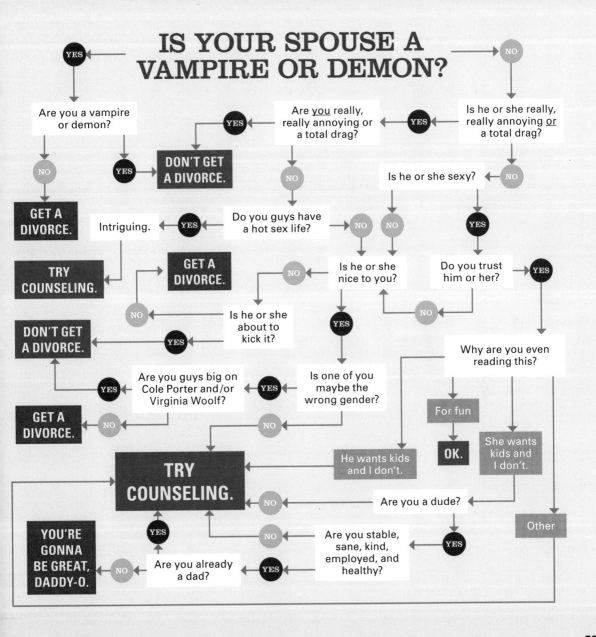

IS YOUR SPOUSE A VAMPIRE OR DEMON?

Am I OLD-FASHIONED?

DO YOU SAY "BRASSIERE"?

CONGRATULATIONS! YOU ARE OLD-FASHIONED. ← YES | NO

"Davenport"? YES | NO

SORRY, YOU ARE NOT OLD-FASHIONED.

Do you take Valium? YES | NO

NO | YES → Do you believe in monogamy?

Do you listen to Johnny Mathis? YES | NO

NO | YES → Do you read the (actual) newspaper?

Do you make popcorn on the stove? YES | NO

NO | YES → Do you knit, crochet, or sew?

Do you smoke Chesterfields? YES | NO

NO | YES → Do you eat Neccos?

Do you have a landline? YES | NO

NO | YES → Do you listen to vinyl LPs?

Do you write checks? YES | NO

NO | YES → Chanel No. 5?

Are you into short-wave radio? YES | NO

NO | YES → Do you wear Old Spice?

Stamp collecting? YES | NO

NO | YES → Do you play (actual) cards?

Jazzercize? YES | NO

NO | YES → Do you use pencils?

Do you drink highballs? YES | NO

NO | YES → Shirley Temples?

Sidecars? YES | NO

Should I

FOLLOW MY DREAMS?

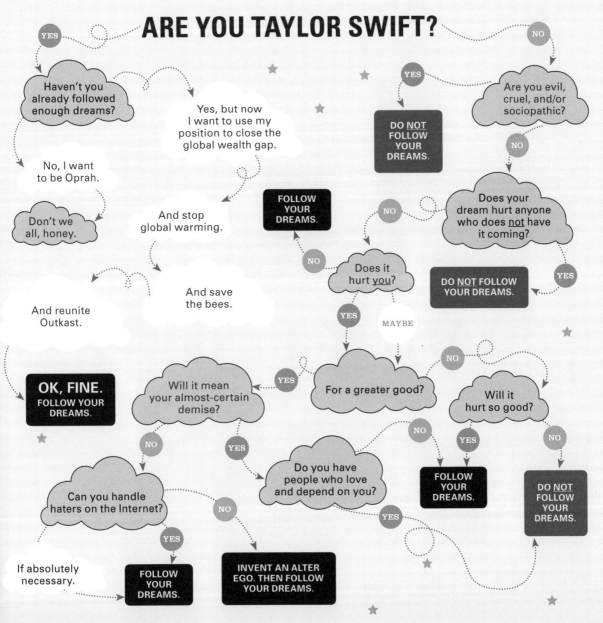

SHOULD WE ELOPE?

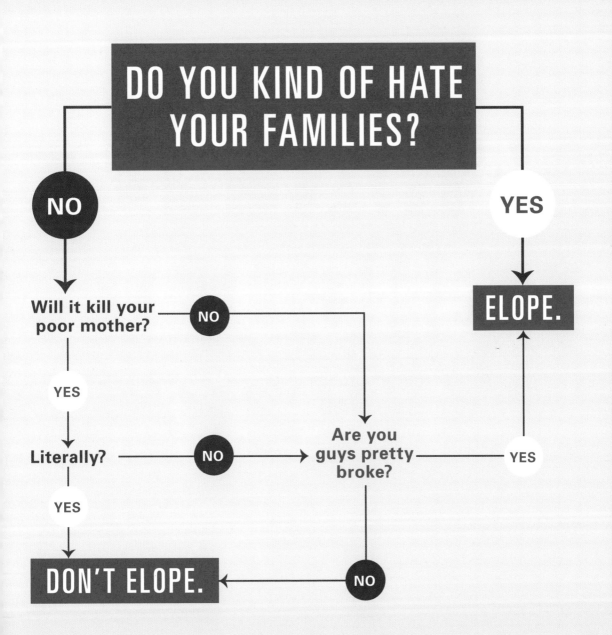

DO YOU KIND OF HATE YOUR FAMILIES?

NO

YES

Will it kill your poor mother?

NO

ELOPE.

YES

Literally?

NO

Are you guys pretty broke?

YES

YES

NO

DON'T ELOPE.

WHAT PET SHOULD I GET?

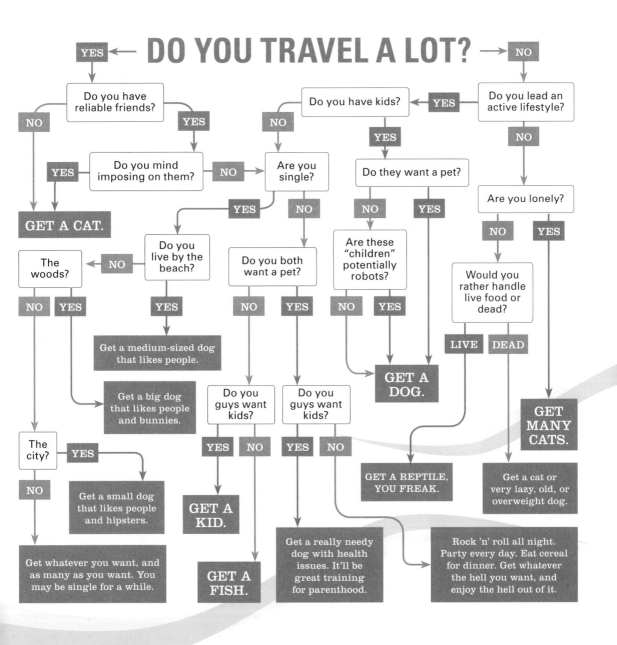

DO YOU TRAVEL A LOT?

YES ← **DO YOU TRAVEL A LOT?** → NO

Do you have reliable friends?
- NO
- YES

Do you lead an active lifestyle?
- YES → **Do you have kids?**
- NO

Do you mind imposing on them?
- YES
- NO → **Are you single?**
  - YES
  - NO

GET A CAT.

Do you live by the beach?
- NO → **The woods?**
- YES

The woods?
- NO
- YES

Do they want a pet?
- NO → **Are these "children" potentially robots?**
- YES

Are you lonely?
- NO → **Would you rather handle live food or dead?**
- YES

Do you both want a pet?
- NO
- YES

Are these "children" potentially robots?
- NO
- YES

Get a medium-sized dog that likes people.

Get a big dog that likes people and bunnies.

Do you guys want kids?
- YES → **GET A KID.**
- NO → **GET A FISH.**

Do you guys want kids?
- YES
- NO

GET A DOG.

Would you rather handle live food or dead?
- LIVE
- DEAD

GET MANY CATS.

The city?
- YES → Get a small dog that likes people and hipsters.
- NO → Get whatever you want, and as many as you want. You may be single for a while.

GET A REPTILE, YOU FREAK.

Get a cat or very lazy, old, or overweight dog.

Get a really needy dog with health issues. It'll be great training for parenthood.

Rock 'n' roll all night. Party every day. Eat cereal for dinner. Get whatever the hell you want, and enjoy the hell out of it.

SHOULD I SWITCH DOCTORS?

AM I
A POET?

WHAT RHYMES WITH "DRESS"?

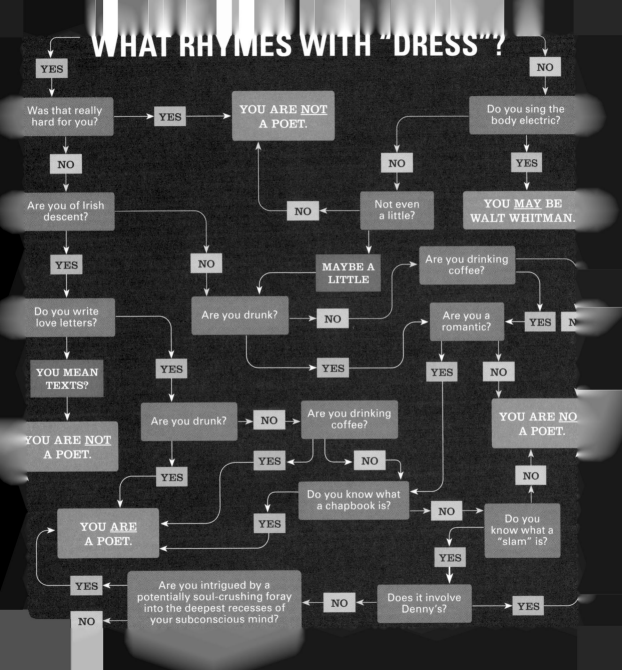

YES

Was that really hard for you? → **YES** → **YOU ARE NOT A POET.**

NO

Are you of Irish descent?

NO

Do you sing the body electric?

YES

Not even a little? → **NO**

YES

YOU MAY BE WALT WHITMAN.

NO

MAYBE A LITTLE

Are you drinking coffee?

YES

Do you write love letters?

NO

Are you drunk? → **NO**

Are you a romantic? → **YES** → N

YES

YOU MEAN TEXTS?

YES

YES

Are you drunk? → **NO** → Are you drinking coffee?

SO **NO**

YOU ARE NOT A POET.

NO

YES

YOU ARE NO A POET.

YES

YOU ARE A POET.

YES

Do you know what a chapbook is? → **NO**

NO

Do you know what a "slam" is?

YES

Are you intrigued by a potentially soul-crushing foray into the deepest recesses of your subconscious mind? → **NO** → Does it involve Denny's? → **YES**

YES

NO

CAN I LIE ON MY ONLINE DATING PROFILE?

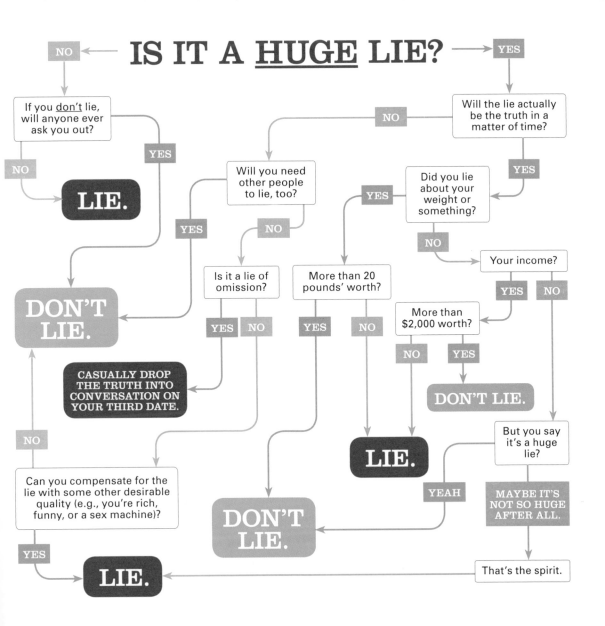

SHOULD I GET A PhD?

DO YOU HAVE A FAVORITE CULTURAL THEORIST?

AM I TOO OUTDOORSY?

ARE YOU OUTSIDE NOW?

NO ← ARE YOU OUTSIDE NOW? → YES

NO:

Are you in a house?

- NO → Are you in an REI?
- YES → Do you live there?
  - YES → Does it have indoor plumbing?
    - NO → YOU ARE TOO OUTDOORSY.
    - YES → YOU ARE NOT TOO OUTDOORSY.
  - NO → Are you stopping by a friend's house to bathe?
    - NO → YOU ARE NOT TOO OUTDOORSY.
    - YES → YOU ARE TOO OUTDOORSY.

Are you in an REI?

- YES → Do you go there often?
  - NO → YOU MAY BE TOO OUTDOORSY.
  - YES → YOU ARE TOO OUTDOORSY.
- NO → Are you doing your biweekly trip to the PO Box?
  - YES → YOU ARE NOT TOO OUTDOORSY.
  - NO → YOU ARE NOT TOO OUTDOORSY.

YES:

Has it been a month or longer since you've seen another person?

- NO → A week?
  - YES → YOU ARE TOO OUTDOORSY.
  - NO → YOU ARE NOT TOO OUTDOORSY.
- YES → Do you have fur, feathers, or scales?
  - NO → YOU ARE NOT TOO OUTDOORSY.
  - YES → YOU ARE NOT TOO OUTDOORSY. YOU ARE A WILD ANIMAL.

SHOULD I MOVE TO LA OR NYC?

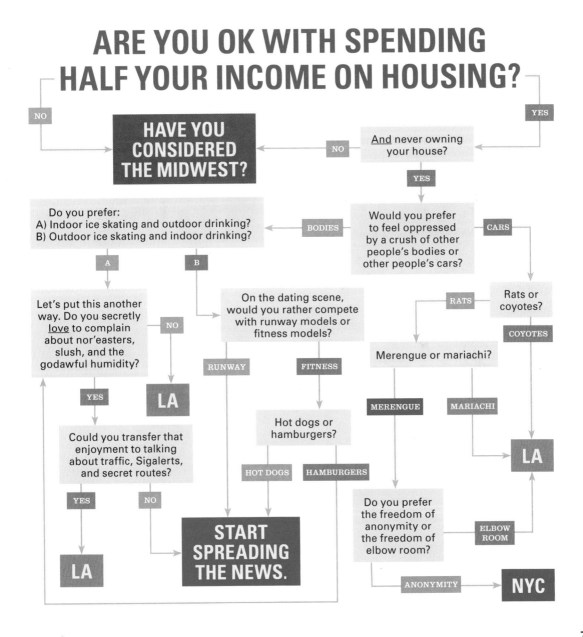

ARE YOU OK WITH SPENDING HALF YOUR INCOME ON HOUSING?

NO

YES

HAVE YOU CONSIDERED THE MIDWEST?

NO

And never owning your house?

YES

Do you prefer:
A) Indoor ice skating and outdoor drinking?
B) Outdoor ice skating and indoor drinking?

BODIES

Would you prefer to feel oppressed by a crush of other people's bodies or other people's cars?

CARS

A

B

Let's put this another way. Do you secretly love to complain about nor'easters, slush, and the godawful humidity?

NO

On the dating scene, would you rather compete with runway models or fitness models?

RATS

Rats or coyotes?

COYOTES

YES

LA

RUNWAY

FITNESS

Merengue or mariachi?

Could you transfer that enjoyment to talking about traffic, Sigalerts, and secret routes?

Hot dogs or hamburgers?

MERENGUE

MARIACHI

YES

NO

HOT DOGS

HAMBURGERS

LA

LA

START SPREADING THE NEWS.

Do you prefer the freedom of anonymity or the freedom of elbow room?

ELBOW ROOM

ANONYMITY

NYC

SHOULD THIS PERSON BE MY BEST MAN / MAID OF HONOR?

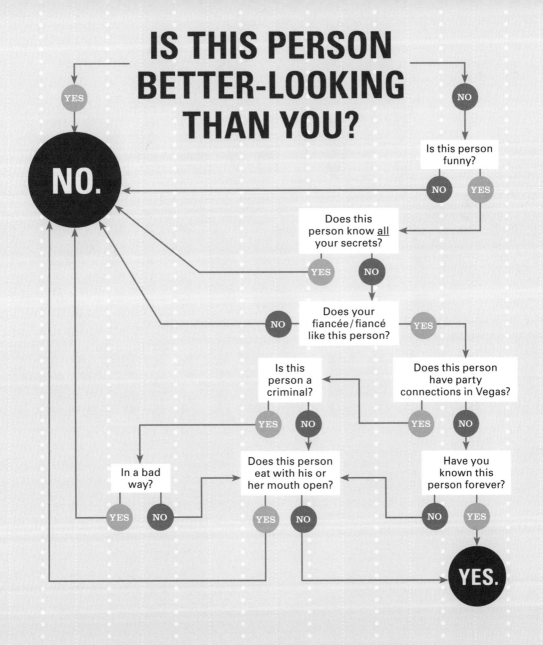

SHOULD I LIKE THIS PICTURE?

IS THIS PICTURE <u>OF</u> OR <u>BY</u> AN EX?

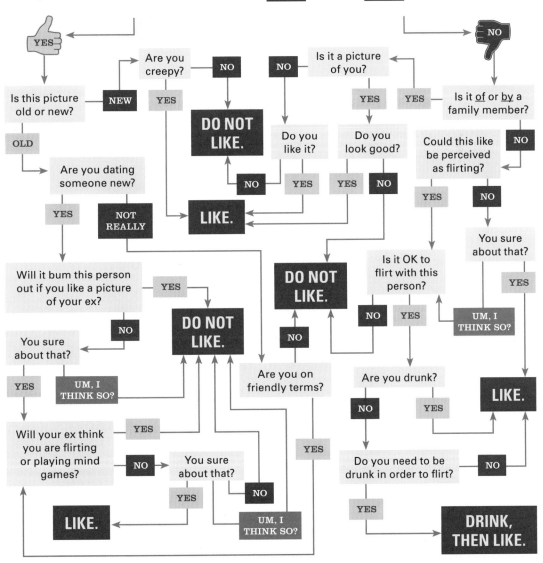

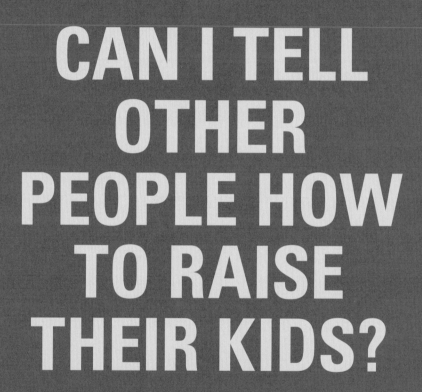

CAN I TELL OTHER PEOPLE HOW TO RAISE THEIR KIDS?

DID THEY ASK FOR YOUR ADVICE?

YES

TELL THEM HOW TO RAISE THEIR KIDS.

YES — Are you legally, professionally, or ethically obliged to tell them how to raise their kids?

YES — Are you a health professional, therapist, social worker, or early childhood expert?

NO

NO

Do you really, really want to anyway?

TELL THEM HOW TO RAISE THEIR KIDS. — **YES** — Are they your parents?

NO

YES

NO

Are they awful people? — **NO** — Are they your kids?

NO

YES

YES

DO NOT TELL THEM HOW TO RAISE THEIR KIDS.

TELL THEM HOW TO RAISE THEIR KIDS.

DO NOT TELL THEM HOW TO RAISE THEIR KIDS.

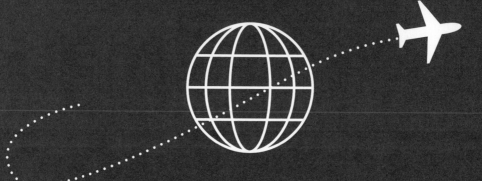

Should I

LEAVE THE
COUNTRY?

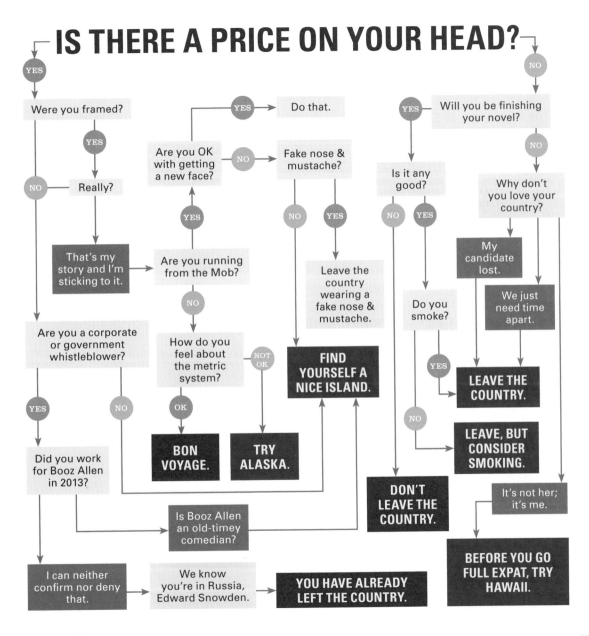

IS THERE A PRICE ON YOUR HEAD?

YES → Were you framed?

Really?

That's my story and I'm sticking to it.

Are you a corporate or government whistleblower?

Did you work for Booz Allen in 2013?

I can neither confirm nor deny that.

YES → Do that.

Are you OK with getting a new face?

Fake nose & mustache?

Are you running from the Mob?

How do you feel about the metric system?

Leave the country wearing a fake nose & mustache.

FIND YOURSELF A NICE ISLAND.

BON VOYAGE.

TRY ALASKA.

Is Booz Allen an old-timey comedian?

We know you're in Russia, Edward Snowden.

YOU HAVE ALREADY LEFT THE COUNTRY.

NO → Will you be finishing your novel?

Is it any good?

Why don't you love your country?

My candidate lost.

We just need time apart.

Do you smoke?

LEAVE THE COUNTRY.

LEAVE, BUT CONSIDER SMOKING.

It's not her; it's me.

DON'T LEAVE THE COUNTRY.

BEFORE YOU GO FULL EXPAT, TRY HAWAII.

87

AM I HAPPY?

DO YOU BELIEVE HAPPINESS IS FOR STUPID PEOPLE?

YES

NO

Do you consider yourself smart?

NO

Do you believe happiness is way overrated?

YES

YES

YOU ARE **NOT** HAPPY.

YOU **ARE** HAPPY.

NO

YES

Do you feel like you have a lot to be grateful for?

Do you feel bad about yourself most of the time?

NO

YES

YOU ARE **NOT** HAPPY.

YES

NO

Is it a cynical laugh?

Do you feel mad, sad, scared, or numb most of the time?

YOU MAY BE UNHAPPY NOW, BUT YOU HAVE GREAT HAPPINESS POTENTIAL.

YES

YES

NO

YOU **ARE** HAPPY.

NO

YES

Do you feel like you don't have very much to be grateful for?

Do you feel grumpy most of the time?

NO

Do you laugh a lot?

NO

NO

YES

Are you evil or maniacal?

YES

Is it an evil or maniacal laugh?

YES

AM I LOVABLE?

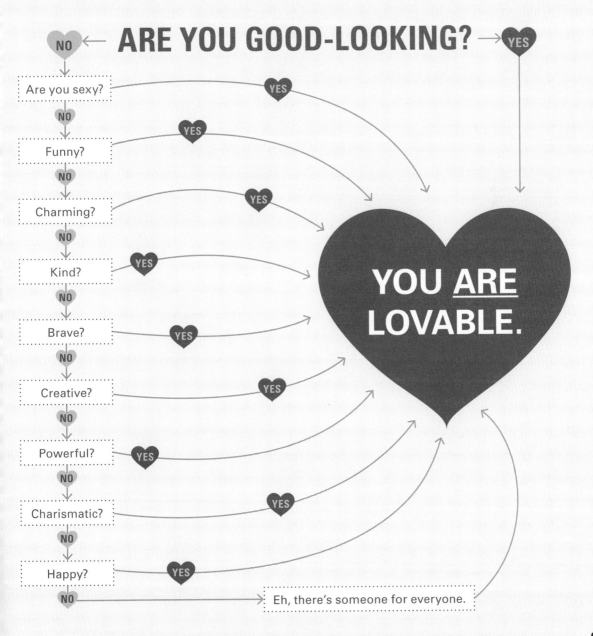

ARE YOU GOOD-LOOKING?

NO → YES

Are you sexy? — YES

Funny? — YES

Charming? — YES

Kind? — YES

Brave? — YES

Creative? — YES

Powerful? — YES

Charismatic? — YES

Happy? — YES

YOU ARE LOVABLE.

NO → Eh, there's someone for everyone.

AM I AN INTROVERT OR EXTROVERT?

DO YOU PREFER CATS, DOGS, OR FISH?

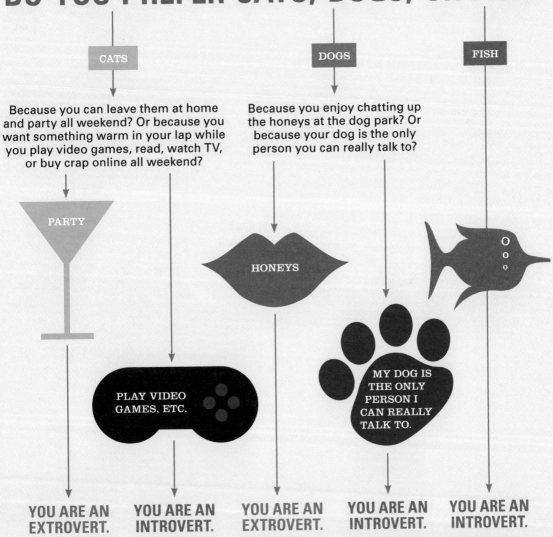

CATS

Because you can leave them at home and party all weekend? Or because you want something warm in your lap while you play video games, read, watch TV, or buy crap online all weekend?

PARTY

PLAY VIDEO GAMES, ETC.

DOGS

Because you enjoy chatting up the honeys at the dog park? Or because your dog is the only person you can really talk to?

HONEYS

MY DOG IS THE ONLY PERSON I CAN REALLY TALK TO.

FISH

O o o

YOU ARE AN EXTROVERT.

YOU ARE AN INTROVERT.

YOU ARE AN EXTROVERT.

YOU ARE AN INTROVERT.

YOU ARE AN INTROVERT.

AM I LEONARD COHEN?

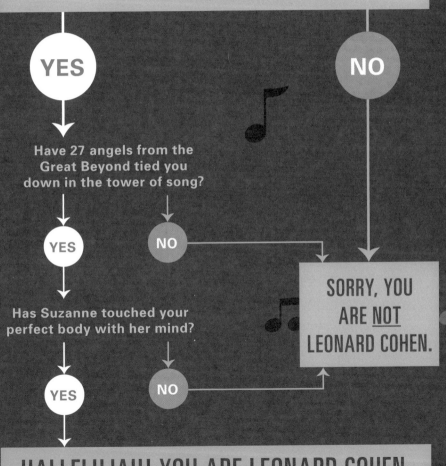